Dyslexia

Dyslexia

Understanding Reading Problems

JOHN F. SAVAGE

Julian Messner  New York

Manufactured in the United States of America
Design by Irving Perkins
Library of Congress Cataloging in Publication Data

Savage, John F., 1938-
Dyslexia: understanding reading problems.

Includes index.
Summary: Describes the characteristics of dyslexia,
its causes, how it affects children, and how these
children can learn to read.
1. Dyslexia—Juvenile literature. [1. Dyslexia]
I. Title.
RC394.W6S28   1985   618.92′8553   85-8925
ISBN 0-671-54289-3

Contents

Acknowledgments

The following people provided information, ideas, and other kinds of help for this book: Ms. Sandy Ardwin, Dr. Charles Drake, Mr. John Green, Mr. Rob Harrington, Mr. Charles Harris, Ms. June Hartel, Ms. Lee Karpa, Ms. Rhonda Phalen, Ms. Linda Rogers, Mr. Matthew Rutter, Dr. David John Smith, Mr. Louis Salza, Mr. Doug Spink, Mrs. Marguerite Tierney, Mr. Scot Wilson. A special note of thanks is due to the staff of the Landmark School in Prides Crossing, Massachusetts.

Before You Read

This book is about *dyslexia*. That word can be difficult to say, to read, and to write. So let's look at the word before starting to read the book.

The word is pronounced dis-LEX-ee-uh. It comes from two old Greek words. The prefix or first part of the word *(dys)* means "lack of" or "being without," or "inadequate." The second part of the word *(lexia)* comes from an old word meaning "word," or "verbal language." The whole word—*dyslexia*—means a problem in learning to read or in learning to deal with language in print. You'll learn a lot more about the meaning of the word as you read this book.

A person who has dyslexia is sometimes known as a *dyslexic*. So a dyslexic boy or a dyslexic girl is a boy or a girl who has dyslexia.

These two words—*dyslexia* and *dyslexic*—will be used again and again throughout this book.

Dyslexia

Chapter 1

The Problem Called Dyslexia

The children went home. The mystery was solved. It had been a wonderful day. The End.

Carl closed the book and put it on his lap. "There. Did you like that story, Julie?" he asked.

"Yes. Read me another. Read me another," his little sister replied.

"No. No more stories tonight," Carl told her.

"Pleeeeez." Julie begged.

"Sorry. Mom said you had to be in bed by eight o'clock. It's ten after eight now. If Mom comes home and you're still up, we'll both be in trouble. She'll yell at you, and she won't let me baby-sit for you any more."

Carl really wanted to read another story, but he knew it was time for Julie to go to bed. He liked to read to his little sister. For one thing, it kept her quiet while he was baby-sitting for her. As long as he was reading, Julie wasn't running around acting hyper. Besides, her books were easy. Carl had no trouble reading them. He wished his books in school were that easy.

"Can I have a glass of juice?" Julie asked.

"Okay. But while I'm getting the juice, you go get Teddy and get into bed. If you're in bed by the time I pour the juice, we'll have more stories tomorrow night."

Julie scurried into her room. By the time Carl walked in with her juice, she was in bed with the covers pulled up to her chin. As she sat up to drink the juice, she made one last try for another story. "Please," she asked. "Just one story before I go to sleep. You're such a good reader, Carl."

Carl wouldn't give in. "Tomorrow night, I told you. Now go to sleep before Mom gets home. Sweet dreams." Carl kissed his little sister good night, snapped off the lights, and went into his own room. He put his favorite record on the stereo, slipped his headset over his ears so that the music would not keep his little sister awake, and sat down to relax.

Carl thought of her words, and he smiled quietly. *You're such a good reader, Carl.*

"If only she knew!" he thought. "I'm now in seventh grade and I'm still getting help with reading. But I am learning, and I'm getting better and better all the time."

Carl, like millions of children in school today, has dyslexia. His teachers call it a learning disability, and it has caused him problems almost since the day he started school.

No one is quite sure how many dyslexic pupils are in our nation's schools. The number is certainly over a million, and it may be as high as ten million. That's not counting the number of children whose problems have not been identified, or the adults in society who have dyslexia. Most are boys. About five times as many boys as girls are learning-disabled. All have trouble learning to read and spell.

Children with dyslexia are, in most ways, just like other children in any school. Dyslexics are not sick. They don't have three eyes or eight toes. They just have more than the normal amount of trouble learning to read and spell.

All children are different. Some are talented artists. Others can't draw a straight line with a ruler. Some sing well. Others can't carry a tune. Some learn long division very quickly. Others take longer to understand. Some can run fast. Others are slowpokes at running. Some love science. Others prefer social studies. Children have different weight and height and eye color and hair color. These individual differences are a fact of life.

Children with dyslexia have these differences as well. Some are good at sports. Others are not. Some like music. Others don't. They may be talented at one thing and clumsy at something else. They may be tall or shor', fat or skinny. Their hair may be blond or black, and their eyes may be brown or blue, just like everybody else. Their eyesight and hearing and physical development may go from very good to very poor. They have the same range of likes and dislikes as anybody else. They have one thing in common. They were born with a learning problem, and this problem causes them difficulties in school.

Children learn lots of different things in school. On the playground, they learn to play games, to make friends, to fight and make up. In gym, they learn to run, to jump, to kick a ball. In the classroom, they learn to read and to write and to spell and to do math.

Some pupils have a natural talent for learning to do these things. Some begin school already knowing how to read and write and count. Others learn to read and write without much effort very early in their school lives. Most must work hard to learn. But for the dyslexic child, this learning is very, very difficult. He or she must make a much greater effort at reading and writing than with learning other things.

For as long as Carl could remember, reading had been difficult for him. In kindergarten, he enjoyed the stories that Mrs. Lamb would read. He loved climbing on the jungle gym with his friend Glen and pushing the little wooden carts around the room at 90 miles an hour. But Carl hated Alphabet Time. He couldn't remember what the letters were called. Thelma called him stupid one day, and so he punched her. She cried, and that made the teacher angry. Another day, he banged the piano during Alphabet Time, and Mrs. Lamb got so mad that she sent him to the principal's office. School wasn't as much fun as he had thought it would be.

First grade wasn't much different. Other kids were learning to read. Glen learned to read a book about horses, and all Carl's friends started to talk about the books they read. Carl worked hard to remember some words in his reading book. But whenever Ms. Marsh asked him to read out loud, Carl made mistakes and the other kids in the group laughed. The harder he tried, the more mistakes he seemed to make. So he stopped trying. He wouldn't read anymore.

At one point or another in their lives, most children have trouble learning or show some sign of a learning problem. Children with dyslexia have more than the average amount of

Reprinted courtesy *Their World 1984*, Foundation for Children with Learning Disabilities, New York City

trouble. There is a great difference between their ability and their achievement, between what they should be capable of learning and what they *are* learning. Dyslexic children constantly lag behind. Their learning problems persist even after their classmates have learned what they are expected to learn.

Children with dyslexia usually get off to a bad start in school. First graders spend most of their time learning to read and write, and this emphasis continues for the next two grades as well. Because reading and writing are major problem areas, dyslexic children experience failure and frustration very early in their school years. They become known as "hard to teach." Teachers tell them to "pay attention." Parents tell them to "try harder." What seems to work well for most children doesn't seem to work for them at all.

When you're growing up, it's not easy to be different from other kids. Children who are different—who have hair that is too long or too short, who dress differently, who like different things—are often called oddballs. It's tough not to fit in. When you're the only one of your friends who can't read, it's doubly difficult. You become the second-class citizen in the group.

Very often, dyslexic children have trouble with classmates. Children can understand some of the more obvious handicaps that they see. Most boys and girls can understand the problems that a deaf or a blind child has. They realize the problems of a child in a wheelchair or on crutches. So children are generally kind and understanding to other children with these physical disabilities.

Unlike physical handicaps, learning disabilities are hidden and are harder to recognize. Dyslexic children appear to be as normal as their classmates. So most of their classmates are not as tolerant and understanding with their less obvious learning problems. Boys and girls can often be cruel to a dyslexic classmate. Because they don't learn to read as easily or as quickly as other children, dyslexic pupils come to be known as "stupid." Because their writing is usually not as neat and they may have trouble staying inside the lines when they color, dyslexic children come to be known as "sloppy." Because they may get extra help from the teacher, their classmates call them "goofy." Because they may bump into other children or disturb others while they should be working, they are called "clumsy."

These names hurt. They lead to bad feelings. Dyslexic children have more than their share of fights on the playground. These fights can be upsetting, because like all boys and girls, children with learning disabilities need as much love and support and friendship as they can get.

When he was in first grade Carl's mother began to suspect that he had a learning problem. And since that time, she had helped him in every way she could.

Like all parents of first graders, Mrs. Taylor proudly and anxiously attended Parents' Night in Carl's first grade classroom. But when she came home, she had lots of questions. Mrs. Taylor asked Carl why none of his papers were on the "Best Work" bulletin board in the front of the room. And she noticed that his name wasn't listed among the "Room Helpers." And his drawings were not among the colorful leaves that were on display in the Science Corner. She wondered why. In a short conversation, Ms. Marsh had used words like "nice boy . . . a little immature . . . lots of energy . . . trouble paying attention . . . was sure he'd come along." It was the kind of stuff that parents and teachers always said to each other the first time they met.

Then first term reports came out and Mrs. Taylor was called to the school for a conference. She met with Ms. Marsh and Mr. Polsky, the school psychologist. The psychologist told her that they suspected that Carl had a learning disability. He said that Carl should be tested. Mrs. Taylor agreed. The test confirmed what the teachers had thought. Carl did have a learning problem, and he would need special help at school.

After that, Mrs. Taylor did everything she could to help Carl. She met regularly with his teachers at school. By quizzing and reviewing with him, she helped him learn his number facts in math and the capitals of all fifty states for social studies. She helped him with his homework every night. She helped him organize his time and plan his work.

Perhaps most important, Mrs. Taylor recognized all the strong points that Carl had. He loved his little sister and was patient and kind in taking care of her. He was the best street hockey player on the block. He was learning to fix things around the house. And once he realized the reason for his difficulties in school, he never stopped trying. That's what Mrs. Taylor liked and admired most about her son. Mrs. Taylor loved Carl very much.

PROBLEMS OF DYSLEXICS

Dyslexia is sometimes called a specific language disability or a specific language difficulty. Language is the central problem for the dyslexic. At different phases of learning language—in learning to speak, to read, to write, and to spell—dyslexic children can have serious difficulty. While each individual case of dyslexia may be different, dyslexics have certain things in common. They have average or above-average intelligence. They have serious difficulty in learning and remembering printed words or symbols. They frequently reverse letters or place them in the wrong order in words.

Doing homework or taking a test may require extra time for a dyslexic pupil. Even if he can read the words on the page, it takes a dyslexic pupil longer to figure out what the words are and to write them.

They make extreme and frequent spelling mistakes. Their handwriting is often close to illegible, and their compositions are poorly written. As a group, dyslexics need specialized teaching that is adjusted to their specific problems and needs.

The learning problems of the dyslexic child very often go beyond difficulties in learning to read and write. Sometimes dyslexic children are forgetful. They forget their pencils or they forget their homework or they forget what they're supposed to do. They may be clumsy in general. Or they may be good at sports but not so good in working with smaller things like pencils or scissors. Dyslexic children often have difficulty organizing their lives. They throw their papers into folders with no order or organization. Their desks may look like a hurricane has just struck. Their idea of time is all mixed up. They have more than the average amount of difficulty sitting still and paying attention. All of this affects their work in the classroom.

Just because a child is forgetful or has a messy desk does not mean that he or she has dyslexia. Every child is different and shows a different combination of learning problems or apparent symptoms of dyslexia. But being forgetful, being disorganized, and having trouble paying attention are all problems that learning-disabled children often have.

Mostly, the dyslexic child's problems are with school subjects. These children have difficulty remembering written words, so they have problems with reading. They can't remember which letters are in a word or the order in which these letters come. So they have great trouble spelling. Sometimes they get letters mixed up, so that *b* looks like *d* and they write *big* for *dig*. They also forget the sequence or order of letters, so that they write *left* when they want to write *felt*.

Problems in reading and writing spread to other school subjects. In math, the child may have trouble remembering number facts or the times tables. The child may confuse number symbols so that 3 and 5 get all mixed up and the number 7 comes out looking like this:

$$f$$

Because of poor organization, the numbers in an addition column may be lined up like this:

```
3 6 2
4 7
  8 69
```

Getting the right answer becomes impossible, not because the child doesn't know how to add, but because the numbers are not lined up the right way. The child may forget to put decimal points in the answers and mix up the top and the bottom of fractions.

Science and social studies become difficult to the extent that they involve reading and writing. Dyslexic pupils have trouble reading and understanding material in the history book. They mix up the directions east and west. They may understand a map but have trouble drawing a neat one. In science, they may understand the content, but they have trouble reading about it. When they try to use a computer like other children, their fingers often hit the wrong keys. So while they know what should be on the screen, they may have trouble getting the right information up there.

By the time dyslexic pupils reach high school, so much reading is required that they are frustrated and handicapped in many of their subjects by their lack of ability at reading and writing.

Read the following story:

Once upon a time there was a beautiful young girl named Cinderella. She lived with her cruel stepmother and two ugly stepsisters.

When the king announced a special ball, Cinderella begged to go. But her stepmother and stepsisters only laughed at her. Cinderella was heartbroken, until her fairy godmother appeared. Her godmother turned a pumpkin into a coach, some mice into horses, and her raggedy dress into a beautiful gown.

Cinderella was the most beautiful girl at the ball. The Prince fell in love with her. Cinderella was having such a good time at the ball that she forgot her godmother's orders to be home by midnight. As the clock struck twelve, Cinderella raced from the ballroom, losing a glass slipper.

The Prince searched the kingdom for his lost love. He ordered his servants to try the glass slipper on every maiden in the land. Finally the servants found Cinderella. The Prince and Cinderella were married and they lived happily ever after.

How did you like it?

This is called *mirror writing*. All the letters in all the words are written backwards. Not all dyslexic people see words in this way. But very often, printed language does appear in reverse to the dyslexic reader.

How would you like to read everything like this?

SUCCESS FOR DYSLEXICS

Children with dyslexia have problems. But they also have lots and lots and lots of strengths, and *they can succeed*. They have to learn to make up for their difficulties. They learn to work around their problems. They learn to build upon the skills that they use well. They earn the respect and understanding of their teachers and their classmates. And they overcome their difficulties with success. They go on to high school. Some go to college and then on to successful jobs.

Many very well known people have had dyslexia. The list is long and impressive: Thomas Edison, the inventor of the light bulb and other famous electric devices; General George Patton, who struggled through the U.S. Military Academy at West Point and became a great military leader; Nelson Rockefeller, who was governor of New York and later vice-president of the United States; Hans Christian Andersen, the brilliant storyteller who gave the world stories like "The Ugly Duckling" and "The Little Mermaid," although he never learned to spell very well. The list goes on.

There are also less famous but successful people in all jobs and in all walks of life—doctors, dentists, lawyers, teachers, engineers, architects—who have dyslexia. These people worked around their problems with print to become very successful in their work.

That's an important point to remember: While dyslexics have problems, they often have tremendous strengths. The secret to their success is to build on these strengths. Even though they may have problems learning to read and write, dyslexics often excel as artists, athletes, mechanics, photographers, or in some other field. Even from a very young age, many successful school and life experiences can be built upon these areas of strength.

By the way, this chapter has been mostly about children with dyslexia and their experiences in school. But dyslexia is not a condition that a person "grows out of." A person doesn't get rid of dyslexia when he or she gets out of school.

There are many dyslexic adults in society. When they were in school, many of these adults were promoted from grade to grade in spite of their reading problems. Some graduated barely able to read. Others found school too difficult and too frustrating, so they dropped out.

Many of these adults hide their learning problems. They are ashamed or embarrassed that they cannot read. Many of them live in fear that they will lose their jobs and not be able to find another because of their reading problems. Some recognize and adjust to their problem, knowing that dyslexia is not something to be ashamed of. They work around their problem and find other means to deal with the demands of reading every day. Some seek help.

This book was written to help you understand dyslexia a little better. It will try to help you understand what people mean when they use many different terms to describe dyslexia. It will explain where dyslexic pupils get in trouble with their language, and it will try to describe some of the school experiences that dyslexic pupils have.

Chapter **2**

Trying to Understand Dyslexia

What do people mean when they say, "Carl has dyslexia"?
Dyslexia is not an easy word to define or explain. Experts
who have studied the subject all their lives don't always agree
on what it is. And as scientists learn more and more about the
brain and how we learn, views about dyslexia change.

At first, the term *dyslexia* was used to refer to reading
problems that were a direct result of brain injury. Many
people still use the term to refer to reading problems that are
caused by a mild defect in the brain. However, people also
use the term much more widely.

For some experts, dyslexia means any and all types of reading problems or difficulties. No matter what the nature or cause of the problem, these experts say that "Carl has dyslexia" whenever Carl has trouble learning to read.

Other authorities link additional problems to the category of dyslexia as well. In these cases, the term is used to describe pupils who have speech problems and other language difficulties, as well as problems in learning how to read. These people use *dyslexia* to refer to pupils with illegible handwriting due to poor hand-eye coordination. They use *dyslexia* when they talk about children who can't sit still for very long, who have trouble paying attention, or who may need extra time to finish their work. These are all problems that often go along with dyslexia, and so the term *dyslexia* is used to include the related problems as well.

Still other experts deny that dyslexia even exists. They admit that some people have a lot of trouble learning to read and write. But these experts object to the use of the word *dyslexia*, and they don't like the fact that the term mixes too many different types of problems. These specialists say that each problem should be identified and described separately, not under one big umbrella called dyslexia. They know the word *dyslexia*, but they refuse to use it.

Even dictionary writers can't get together on a meaning for the word. Different dictionaries give different definitions of the term. Here are three definitions of the word *dyslexia*:

> from *The Random House Dictionary of the English Language*:
> an impairment (problem) of the ability to read due to a brain defect
>
> from *Webster's Third International Dictionary*:
> a disturbance of the ability to read

from *The Oxford English Dictionary*:
> a difficulty in reading due to affection (influence) of the brain

Some dictionaries don't include the word at all.

So when somebody says, "Carl has dyslexia," it can mean a number of different things to different people. These different definitions of the word often cause confusion. Two people talking about dyslexia may not be talking about the same problem. That's why so many other terms are so often used in place of the word *dyslexia*. The different definitions also lead to trouble in estimating the number of people who have dyslexia. The estimated number can range from less than a million to more than ten million. If dyslexia is defined simply as "a reading problem," then there are certainly many more dyslexics than those whose reading problem is "due to a brain defect."

If the experts can't quite agree on a definition of the word, what can they agree on? Most people agree that:

1. Dyslexia is a condition that causes problems in learning how to read and write.

Dyslexia is a language problem. Dyslexics typically have trouble trying to read and write the symbols of their language system. Dyslexia may or may not involve problems with spoken language. But it always involves problems with print.

Problems in learning language can lead to many other problems in school. Success in the classroom depends a lot on reading and writing. The more important reading becomes in a pupil's school life, the more the problems grow and the more complicated the problems become.

2. Dyslexia is not related to intelligence.

In general, dyslexics have average or above-average intelligence. They are not retarded. Their learning problems are not due to low intelligence. In fact, they may be brilliant thinkers with very bright ideas.

Problems with reading and writing may get in the way of progress in school. Dyslexic pupils may be seen as "not being too bright" because of the difficulty they have in dealing with print. That's why teachers sometimes let dyslexic pupils listen to a story instead of reading it. And sometimes dyslexic pupils can dictate a story instead of writing it themselves. Then the dyslexic pupils often show their intellectual ability and knowledge.

3. Dyslexia is not caused by poor vision or poor hearing.

In general, dyslexics see and hear adequately. Their reading problems are not due to problems with the senses of sight or hearing. Some may wear glasses and some may have a little problem hearing, but this is also true of many other children who don't have trouble learning to read. While it is possible that a deaf or a blind person may also have dyslexia, most pupils with dyslexia see and hear quite well.

Dyslexia is often connected with a perceptual problem. That is, the dyslexic pupil sees symbols and hears sounds clearly, but these symbols and sounds do not register properly in the brain. This is very different from not being able to see and hear clearly. (This problem of perception will be explained a little later in this chapter.)

4. Dyslexia does not come from any emotional block to learning.

Dyslexics do not have learning problems because they are

A student with dyslexia can usually see words on the chalkboard. But when she tries to copy or write these words, a dyslexic pupil can have great difficulty getting the words correct on her own paper.

emotionally disturbed. Some may develop emotional problems as a result of the unusual difficulties they meet in trying to learn to read and write. Although they try hard, they fail. So they become angry and frustrated. As a result of unhappy experiences in school, problems in dealing with others develop.

It's important to remember, however, that these emotional problems are the *result* of learning problems, not the cause of learning problems for the dyslexic pupil.

A dyslexic, then, is a person who has trouble learning to read and write. He or she has these problems in spite of generally normal intelligence and no unusual physical or emotional problems. He or she fails in school because reading, writing, and spelling skills have not yet caught up with his or her thinking and problem-solving abilities.

Coming to this fairly sharp and precise definition of dyslexia is important for two reasons. First, it's important that dyslexic pupils understand why they have trouble learning to read. When people know about problems they have, then they have a better chance of understanding the problem, relating to it, and doing something about it. Second, it's important that schools understand the problem. When schools define dyslexia in this precise way, pupils with dyslexia will more likely be placed in the correct type of educational program. Understanding the problem should prevent schools from placing dyslexic pupils with children having different types of learning and behavior problems. When placed in these "mixed" settings, dyslexic pupils may begin imitating some of the behavior problems that they see around them.

Dyslexia is not a disease. It can't be cured like an ear infection. It can't be fixed like a broken leg. It won't go away like chicken pox or a common cold. Dyslexia is a condition.

It's a condition that must be dealt with. It's a condition that requires certain changes in the person's school life in learning to read and write.

DIFFERENT TERMS FOR DYSLEXIA

While the word *dyslexia* has been around for a long time, many other terms have also been used to name the learning problems that dyslexic people have.

In 1966, a government committee investigated the problem of dyslexia. The committee's report contained over twenty terms for dyslexia and related learning problems. Some of the terms that the committee used were *learning disability* or *specific learning disability*, *minimally brain damaged* or *neurologically impaired*, and *perceptually handicapped*.

All of these terms are often used by people today. Each term tells a little bit about the problem that the dyslexic person has. But none of these terms tells the whole story or satisfies everyone.

Let's look at some of these terms to see what the terms mean and to see why people use these terms instead of the word *dyslexia*.

Learning Disability or Specific Learning Disability

"Learning disability"—or LD—is a fairly recent term. It is most often used by people who work in schools: teachers, principals, tutors, school psychologists, and others who work with children in an educational setting. Why did school people start to use the term "learning disabilities?" Because their major job is helping children learn, teachers began to describe children's problems as learning problems. They were concerned with factors that got in the way of learning in school.

In the old days, before schools knew or cared as much about children as they do now, anyone who had trouble learning was just considered stupid. These children were usually called lazy. They were often beaten or punished in some other way. And if they still didn't learn, they had to repeat the same grade year after year.

School became a very unhappy place for these children. They skipped school as much as possible and sometimes became troublemakers. And they usually left school, or dropped out, as soon as they could.

Schools then began to become more aware of some of the problems that many children had. Special schools and special programs were set up for children who were blind, deaf, mentally retarded, or emotionally disturbed. The field of Special Education grew. But teachers recognized that there was still a group of children who had none of these "special" problems but who still had difficulty learning. These children had problems of various kinds. Yet they didn't fit into any neat category like "mentally retarded" or "emotionally disturbed."

In 1963, Dr. Samuel Kirk, a leader in the field of Special Education, suggested the term *learning disabilities*. Because many school people found the word *dyslexia* too general or too technical, these educators began to use the term *learning disabilities* to refer to children who had no serious mental, emotional, or physical problem but who still had trouble in learning to read.

When they work with children, learning-disabilities teachers try to find the exact source of a child's learning problem.

Different terms are used for *dyslexia*—minimal brain damage, learning disability, perceptual handicap. Whatever you call it, dyslexia means that pupils have extra trouble learning to read and write. It also means that dyslexic pupils need extra help from their friends and teachers at school.

Thus the term *specific*, which means exact or precise, is often added to the term *learning disabilities*.

Minimally Brain Damaged

To many people, the expression *brain damaged* sounds terrible. Some people become frightened when they hear it. Even when the word *minimally*—which means "only slightly"—is added, people become alarmed by the term. They think that someone who is brain damaged is insane or retarded. But that is not true. The term is not as bad as it sounds.

What does *minimal brain damage* mean?

The brain is the message center of the human body. All the information that we receive through our eyes, our ears, and our other sense organs is sent to the brain. In the brain, this information is sorted, interpreted, organized, filed away in our memory, or treated in some other way.

The human brain is made up of millions and millions of tiny cells. It consists of about three pounds of soft, delicate tissue. Running through this tissue is a complicated network of millions—or maybe billions—of tiny nerve fibers. Although relatively small, the brain is an amazingly complex and powerful machine, more complex and powerful than any computer or other machine invented by humans.

Neurologists—scientists who study the brain—have found that the brain is divided into several different parts. Each part has a different function, or does a different job. For example, one part of the brain controls the very precise movements that an artist uses as he or she draws. Another area of the brain is tied to memory; an injury to that part of the brain influences how well we remember what we learn.

Nerve fibers connect all the parts so that the brain works as a single unit.

Language—including listening, speaking, reading, and writing—is handled by the left hemisphere, or the left half of the brain. That is, when you hear a spoken word or see a written word, the word "registers" in a section on the left-hand side of the brain. Other nonlanguage and visual messages—like art and music, for example—are handled in the right hemisphere, or the right half of the brain. In the dyslexic, these left-side language areas don't seem to work as well as the right side. This explains why a dyslexic is often excellent in activities like art, architecture, photography, mechanics, or athletics, even though he or she may have great difficulty in reading, writing, spelling, or even in math.

Another thing that scientists learned about the brain is that information taken in on one side of the body is immediately sent to the opposite side of the brain. Thus, if you touch something hot with your left hand, the sensation immediately travels to the right side of the brain. If you feel a bug crawling on your left foot, this sensation goes first to the right side of the brain. Both sides of the brain, of course, send messages back and forth between hemispheres in a split second. Even though different parts do different things, the brain works as a single unit.

How do neurologists find out about the different jobs that various parts of the brain do? They can't take out a person's brain to see language going into one part and music going into another. So how do they know that language is handled in the left hemisphere?

For many years, scientists have studied the actions of people whose brains have been injured in war, in car crashes, or in other accidents. Over a hundred years ago, doctors began to notice that when damage was done to the left side of the brain, the person's language ability was disturbed. Language skills were not as badly affected when the damage was done to the right hemisphere, or right side of the brain. These early discoveries led brain scientists to suspect that the left side of the brain had a lot to do with learning and using language. Later research confirmed these discoveries. Doctors were able to pinpoint areas of the human brain in which language was processed.

Scientists have also devised a special kind of listening test called *dichotic listening*. The person being tested wears earphones. Then two different noises are presented at the same time into the listener's ears. For example, the word *dog* may be spoken into the left ear and the word *cat* said into the right ear. The listener has to repeat the word or sound that he or she hears.

When given this test, people almost always repeat the words or sounds they hear through their right ear. Remember, information from the right side of the body goes first to the left side of the brain. The signal that comes in through the right ear goes immediately to the left side of the brain. The message that first gets to the speech and language area in the left hemisphere is the message that the brain quickly processes and remembers. That's because the left hemisphere is more vital for speech and language. Because dyslexia is a problem dealing with language—that is, reading and writing—scientists suspect that dyslexia may involve a problem with processing language in the brain. Thus, the term *minimal brain damage* is used.

The fact that information goes from the right side of the body to the left side of the brain and vice versa also explains another common belief about dyslexia. People have believed that dyslexia was linked to the fact that the two hemispheres of the brain didn't work together the way they should.

Humans are usually either right-handed or left-handed. A few are ambidextrous; that is, they can use both hands equally well. But most of us prefer to use one hand or the other. The same goes for the eyes and the feet. Most people who are right-handed prefer to kick a ball with their right foot and to use their right eye when they look through a telescope or a microscope. Someone who is left-handed normally prefers to use the leg, foot, and eye on the left side of the body.

One side of the body is said to be *dominant*. That is, either the right or the left side is more important or more influential than the other side. Limbs on that side of the body are used more often and more easily. Because one side of the body is dominant, the opposite side of the brain is considered dominant.

For many years, the issue of brain dominance was linked to the problem of dyslexia. Experts believed that mixed dominance—the tendency to throw a ball with the left hand but to kick a ball with the right foot, for example—was tied to dyslexia. No one side of the body was used all the time. No one hemisphere of the brain was considered dominant. The expressions *mixed dominance* or *incomplete dominance* were used to describe this situation.

Some experts believed that this mixed dominance caused the reading problems that dyslexic pupils had. Because the left or right hemisphere was not dominant, these people said dyslexic learners sometimes saw words backwards. For example, they mixed up *was* and *saw*. The symbols became twisted or all mixed up.

This belief about the cause of dyslexia led to a particular kind of treatment. Pupils' reading problems were treated by having pupils do exercises using only one side of the body or the other. The purpose of these exercises was to make only one hemisphere the dominant hemisphere of the brain. People believed that this would correct the pupils' mixed dominance, and thus correct the reading problems that they believed were the result of the condition.

Medical and educational experts are now more cautious about this theory. Their research has led them to question this belief. The relationship between handedness and brain dominance is not as clear as it once seemed to be. Many pupils without learning problems show mixed dominance, and many learning-disabled pupils show strong preference for the same side of the body all the time.

Neurologists are also using computers and other modern equipment to find out more about the human brain and how it works. Brain waves, or signals that the brain sends out, are measured by electricity. These brain waves can be used to make "maps" of the brain to show how it looks and how it operates.

Medical researchers have found that these "brain maps" show some very slight differences in the language areas in the brains of dyslexic people. The brain cells in areas important to language are formed just a little differently. There's a different pattern or organization, a different "look" about these parts of the brain. These differences may account for the dyslexic person's difficulty in dealing with printed language.

The term *brain damage* to describe dyslexia is most often used by doctors and other medical people. These medical professionals see dyslexia as a brain-based problem, just as school people see dyslexia as a learning disability because their job involves helping children learn.

A lot of study and investigation is still going on, and

scientists still have a lot to learn about the human brain and how it works. The more scientists learn, however, the better will be our chances of solving some of the riddles of dyslexia. More information may lead to a better understanding of dyslexia and how to treat the learning problems connected to it. But in the meantime, we are left with the terrible-sounding term *brain damage*.

Neurologically Impaired

An expression closely related to *brain damaged* is *neurologically impaired*. The meaning of the two expressions is very similar.

The neurological system—or central nervous system—is made up of the brain, the spinal cord, and bundles of nerve fibers that run to and from all parts of the body. This very complicated network or system carries messages between the brain and the various parts of the body. Nerve fibers act like wires that carry electricity all over a house. Some nerve fibers carry information to the brain from all over the body. Other nerve fibers carry messages from the brain to different parts of the body. And still other fibers link or join the various parts of the central nervous system.

In dyslexic people, some of these messages may get a little mixed up. There can be a "short circuit" as the information travels within the central nervous system. Some of these "wires" may be crossed, or connected improperly, or not connected at all where they should be. Thus, there can be a problem as the image of a printed symbol goes from the eye to the brain. Or the sounds in a spoken word don't get sent properly from the ear to the brain. Or the hand does not get the correct message from the brain about writing a word. Or the person has trouble reading or writing words he or she sees.

Because these problems happen within the neurological system, dyslexic people are sometimes said to be *neurologically impaired*. And because the brain is the main message center of the central nervous system, the term is closely related to the expression *brain damaged*.

Perceptually Handicapped

In order to try to understand the meaning of the expression *perceptually handicapped*, let's look at the meaning of each word separately.

Let's take the easy one first, *handicapped*. A handicap is a condition that makes success more difficult. A person who is handicapped usually has more trouble than the average person. (It's important to recognize, however, that many handicapped people overcome their handicaps and accomplish great things.) Normally, a handicap is a disability that causes a disadvantage. A perceptual handicap causes difficulty in a person's perception.

Now, what does *perception* mean? Perception is the correct interpretation of signals that come in through the eyes, the ears, and the other senses. We receive information through our senses. This information is then carried to the brain by the bundles of nerve fibers that were described in the last section, those "wires" that are part of the central nervous system. Meaning is attached to this information when the brain selects, organizes, and interprets the signals it receives. The brain integrates, or puts together, all this information into an awareness of what is seen and heard. This is the process of perception. It all happens in a split second.

Perception is more than the ability to see or hear. It's the ability to attach meaning to what we see and hear (and taste, touch, and smell, too). For example, you may see the symbol *b* or the sequence of the letters STAR properly. Or you may hear the sounds of the word *girl* perfectly well. But if you perceive the symbol *b* as *d* or *p*, or if you perceive the sequence of letters in STAR as RATS, or if the sounds of *girl* register as *gril*, then you're bound to have trouble reading. These are the types of perceptual problems that handicap the dyslexic person in learning to read.

Perception involves a number of different activities. It involves an awareness of likenesses and differences in the size, shape, direction, color, and other qualities of the visual symbols we see. These visual symbols include the letters of the alphabet we need to recognize in learning to read. Perception also involves an awareness of the likenesses and differences in the sounds we hear. The relationship of these sounds includes the sounds we hear in words. Perception also includes the ability to pick out one sound or one symbol from all the sounds and symbols around it.

This is all part of perception. People who can't do all these things quickly and easily are said to be perceptually handicapped.

The expressions described here—learning disabled, minimally brain damaged, neurologically impaired, and perceptually handicapped—are not the only terms or labels attached to the dyslexic. Some people see the physical aspects of the problem and name it by those aspects. Others see the educational dimensions of the problem and call it by another name. Other terms are used as well. But these four expressions seem to be the ones most commonly used.

No matter what the condition is called, the effects of dyslexia are the same. In spite of normal or above-average intelligence, problems in learning to read and write occur.

The brain seems to play tricks. Children who never had trouble learning anything now have difficulty learning to read and spell. Children who could understand and remember stories now can't seem to remember letters or words. Children who can understand what they experience in their worlds have to struggle to understand language that is written down. These children see classmates moving ahead in school while they are kept back. It's easy to understand why they get so frustrated and angry.

Dyslexia is a condition that causes problems. That's why it's important to understand it and to do something about the problems it causes rather than just trying to put a name or a label on it.

Chapter 3

Understanding Language

People with dyslexia have trouble with language. They sometimes have trouble with spoken words. They always have trouble with language in its written form, trouble in reading and writing language that is written down. In fact, dyslexia is sometimes called a specific *language* disability. So in order to understand more about dyslexia, it will be helpful to understand a little about language and how we learn it.

SPEECH AND WRITING

Speech is the first form of language. Humans were using speech thousands and thousands of years before writing was ever invented. Nobody is sure how language started. Some people believe that language began as people expressed emotions like fear and joy. Others say that language originated as people imitated the natural sounds they heard around them, like the cry of a bird or the roar of a storm. Many people believe that language develops as part of a person's intelligence. While we still don't know who invented language, we do know that no group of people ever lived without using language to communicate with one another.

People do know how writing started. Prehistoric people drew rough drawings on the walls of the caves where they lived. Some of these drawings can still be seen today. The ancient Egyptians changed some of these pictures to symbols—called hieroglyphics—that stood for objects and ideas. Gradually, these hieroglyphics began to represent spoken sounds. These symbols were borrowed and changed a lot by the Greeks and the Romans, but they were the beginning of the letters that you're looking at right now as you read.

Speaking and Listening. The process of learning spoken language starts the day we are born. Infants cry when they are unhappy or wet, and they babble and coo when they are content. These baby sounds are the beginnings of communication through language. Babies all over the world, no matter what language they will grow up speaking, make these same sounds at the same time in their first year of life. Then babies start making the single sounds that make up the language they will learn to speak.

Soon, the baby puts sounds together into simple familiar words like *mama* or *doggie*. The child's parents and others begin to understand what he or she is saying. At first, children use the same word to name many similar things; for example, all animals are called *doggie*, from the elephant in the zoo to the pet mouse in a cage. Gradually, children learn to call things by their right names.

As they learn to speak, young children learn the language that is spoken around them. As the English-speaking child learns to say *dog*, the French child learns *chien*, the Spanish child learns *perro*, and the German child learns *hund*. Children even pick up the accents or dialects from their own environments.

Very soon after they learn to speak, small children learn to put words together into little sentences like "Want cookie" or "Daddy bye-bye." These little sentences grow into larger ones, so that by the age of three or four, most children are using spoken language to communicate with everyone around them.

At the same time as they are learning to speak, children learn to understand words that are spoken to them. Little children can understand simple commands or directions like "Get in the car," simple questions like "Where's Teddy?" and simple statements like "Billy will be home soon" long before they can speak these sentences. As they get older and older, they learn to understand longer sentences and stories like "The Three Little Pigs" and "Little Red Riding Hood." Their listening power grows along with their ability to speak.

All of this language learning that you did in the very early years of life was done easily and automatically. You learned language on a certain schedule, so that by the time you came to school, you could use it to send and receive messages, to tell people what was on your mind, and to understand them when they spoke to you.

Most children with dyslexia learn to speak and listen at the same time and in the same way as all other children. They don't run into problems until they meet print in school in reading and writing. Some dyslexic boys and girls, however, encounter problems learning language at a very early age. These children are slower than normal in learning language. Their language development is delayed. They don't begin talking at the same time as other children. They have difficulty understanding the meaning of words. Their speaking vocabulary remains limited. They have difficulty in expressing their needs and in communicating their ideas. These problems cause children great frustration. In some cases, the problems are still present when the child is old enough to go to school.

These problems with spoken language cause additional problems in the classroom. The children have trouble expressing themselves. Even when they know the answer, they may not be able to use the right word when asked. The problems carry over into reading as well. Because the vocabulary of these children is limited, they can't understand the meaning of many of the words in their reading books. That's why, for these children, educational programs often need to go back to the very beginning steps of language development.

It is important to realize that not all dyslexic children have these problems in learning to speak or in using oral language in school. Some do. But the majority of children with dyslexia learn to listen and speak and communicate "on schedule" in their early years of life, before they come to school. For most children with dyslexia, their learning disability becomes apparent when they bump into language in print.

Reading and Writing. Speech sounds are written down. We use the letters of the alphabet to write down the sounds we speak. First we learn to combine the sounds in the spoken word *dog*. Then we learn to use the three letters *d-o-g* to represent that spoken word in writing.

When we see these three written symbols on a page and know what they mean, we are in the first stages of reading. This process of figuring out what written symbols mean in words is called *decoding*. We write words by writing the letters to represent the sounds in the words we want to use. This process is called *encoding*.

For most children, learning to encode and decode written language begins the day they start school. Some children may already be able to say and write the letters in their names. Others may be able to read a few words before they come to school. But almost all children get into reading and writing when they start school for the first time. And this is when the dyslexic pupil first starts to have problems.

While all dyslexic pupils are not alike and they may have different problems in reading and writing, they almost always have great difficulty connecting the sounds and symbols of their language. The kindergarten teacher teaches the alphabet, but the dyslexic child might perceive the shape of the letters differently. These children may not remember the name of a letter. Or they may not remember the sound that it makes. Or they may have trouble remembering how to write it. And when they do copy it, they may write it very sloppily.

The first grade teacher shows the children a word and teaches them how to read it. To the dyslexic child, the word may look different than it looks to other children in the group. The child may not be able to remember what the word is or what it looks like. For the dyslexic child, the letters in the word might look all mixed up. And as other children in the group learn more and more words, the dyslexic child falls further and further behind.

The first grade teacher asks pupils to spell words. The

dyslexic child may have trouble getting the sounds in the word correct, or may have trouble remembering the letters for those sounds, or may have trouble making the right movements to write these letters. In writing, dyslexic children almost always have difficulty getting the letters in the proper order and making sure all the correct letters are there. The more words they have to spell, the bigger the problem becomes.

From the early stages of school, problems develop and increase in reading and writing, and so the child is said to have dyslexia.

FOUR BASIC STEPS IN THE LEARNING PROCESS

In order to better understand some of the specific problems that dyslexic people face in learning to read and write, let's look at the four basic steps in the learning process. The four steps include: (1) Input, (2) Integration, (3) Memory, and (4) Output. Each step is very important to learning in school.

Input. All learning starts with the five senses: seeing, hearing, feeling, tasting, and smelling. Through our five senses, we pick up information from the world around us. Through our eyes we see color, shape, form, and other visual features of objects around us. Our ears tell us whether sounds are loud or soft, high or low, pleasant or unpleasant. Our sense of feeling lets us know if an object is hot or cold, smooth or rough, hard or soft. Taste and smell tell us when food or odors are sweet or sour, pleasant or unpleasant. Each of these senses is the start of a pathway to the brain.

Reading programs for dyslexic pupils stress phonics. Pupils can already say the sounds of their language. They learn the letters for these sounds so that they can "sound out" words in reading.

The sensory organs are attached to the central nervous system, which contains the nerves that send this information to the brain. The brain is the message center of the body. The brain is where the next step in the learning process takes place.

Integration. Like a giant computer, the brain sorts through all the information it receives through the senses. It puts the information in the right order, organizes it, and integrates it along with other bits of information so that it gets meaning out of the message. For example, the ear picks up the sound of a bell and passes it along to the brain. The brain recognizes the sound as a telephone bell (as opposed to a doorbell or a school bell) and sends the mental message back, "Answer the phone."

Memory. The third step in the learning process is memory. The brain receives information and attaches meaning to it. Then the brain stores the information in the person's memory so that the person can use the information when it is needed again. Memory plays a very important part in what pupils have to learn in school.

Output. Information stored in the memory can be produced. It is called output. We use output to answer the questions that the teacher asks. The output is sometimes verbal and sometimes motor. In other words, we sometimes say the answer, or sometimes we show the answer through moving or by pointing.

In any one of these four steps, the dyslexic can experience a great deal of difficulty.

Even when the sensory organ receives the message correctly, the message can get garbled in the *input* and *integra-*

tion stages of learning. Here's where the *b* is seen as a *d*, where *was* is perceived as *saw*, where *3* is seen as *E*. Left and right are often mixed up. Words and lines are skipped in reading. Depth perception is distorted, so that the child may knock things over or bump into people. Letters get mixed up in spelling. All the letters may be there, but they are often in the wrong order. Information is organized awkwardly, so that events in a story are all mixed up and the sequence in a simple set of directions is not followed correctly. All of these problems cause difficulties in reading and writing.

Dyslexic learners often have more than the normal amount of trouble getting information out of their *memory*. A frequent expression is "I forgot." They forget quickly. They have trouble remembering what to call letters and words. They frequently forget things like their pencil, their phone number, or their homework. They may not be able to recall a word for an answer, even though they know the word and its meaning. They have trouble remembering what happened in a story.

The final step in the learning process, *output*, can cause trouble for the dyslexic, too. Handwriting is typically very sloppy, so sloppy that it can be almost impossible to read. So even though the pupil's ideas are excellent and the answers are perfect, he or she has unusual difficulties expressing these ideas and answers in writing. Motor output can cause problems in kicking a ball or skipping, too. Responding to questions can be a particular problem.

Not all dyslexics, of course, have problems in the same areas of learning. For some, understanding spoken language may not be a problem, but integrating and remembering information may be weak areas. For others, integration and memory may be all right, but written output may be a real problem. Separating these problem areas in learning is part

I had aen aksidant. I was
faloing Jeff on my Bike
and I RAN inot de Car I
was scared Belus I Thot
my leg was Broken but
it wasnt. It was onley
a little BrusED,

This sample of handwriting shows some of the problems that learning-disabled children can have putting their ideas into writing. Words are often spelled just the way they sound (*aksidant*). Easy words are mis-spelled (*onley*). Letters are reversed in words (*inot*). The handwriting is so poor that it is very difficult to read.

of the task of understanding and dealing with dyslexia. Trying to identify the exact source of the problem, some experts use the term *specific learning disability* or *specific language disability* instead of *dyslexia*.

UNDERSTANDING PROBLEMS OF DYSLEXICS

If a person perceives the sounds and symbols of language incorrectly, then these sounds and symbols are bound to come out incorrectly in reading and writing. People don't learn in separate, isolated compartments. Their minds function as whole units. Trying to figure out exactly where the difficulty is and trying to deal with it is part of the problem of understanding and treating dyslexia.

It's also important to remember that because you sometimes have some of these problems, you don't automatically have dyslexia. Little children often spell words backwards because they still don't know that printed language goes from left to right in English. All children—even the most capable—forget their pencils or their homework sometimes. And just because your mother tells you that your handwriting is sloppy or you fail a spelling test once in a while doesn't mean you have dyslexia. Everyone has these problems. The dyslexic person has more than his or her share of these problems, however. The problems become so serious that success in school becomes unusually difficult.

Problems that the dyslexic pupil encounters at each step of the learning process are subtle and often mysterious. They are in some ways like problems in music and art. Some people hear and enjoy music greatly, but they can't sing or play a note. They hear the notes that Frank Sinatra sings or that the Rolling Stones play, but they lack the talent to reproduce those notes themselves. Other people know and appreciate art. They can recognize and describe the works of the masters, but when they try to draw something themselves, the results are funny.

Society tends to accept these limitations that people have in learning art and music. But people are less patient and understanding in dealing with the problems that the dyslexic faces. The dyslexic person has problems learning language. He or she hears the sounds and sees the symbols but has trouble producing these sounds and symbols in reading and writing. Because the causes are not obvious, the problems are frequently misunderstood by teachers, parents, and classmates.

Because of their problems and the misunderstandings that result, the dyslexic person frequently becomes frustrated. Learning problems lead to broader problems in dealing with others. It has been found that more than one-third of the boys who are judged delinquent by courts have some form of learning disability.

Does that mean that pupils with dyslexia are doomed to a life of failure and frsutration? Of course not! It does emphasize, however, the importance of trying to better understand the difficulties that dyslexic pupils face in trying to learn to read and write. It emphasizes the need to recognize the problems and provide special instruction that will help the dyslexic pupil. It emphasizes the importance of recognizing and building upon the strengths that dyslexic pupils have.

Chapter 4

Teaching Dyslexic Pupils

Schools are in the business of helping all pupils learn. This business includes pupils who learn easily as well as those who don't. Dyslexic pupils learn differently—and usually with a lot more difficulty—than other children in school. Therefore, there will probably be differences in the school programs of dyslexic pupils. The school's job is to help pupils learn the information and develop the skills that will help them succeed in school and in later life. For the dyslexic pupil, the school program may need to be changed according to the pupil's needs.

These changes in the pupil's school routine should be accepted, just as adjustments for other handicaps are generally accepted by other pupils. No one would expect a pupil in a wheelchair to climb stairs or a blind pupil to read what's written on the chalkboard. So no one should expect a dyslexic learner to go through a regular school routine without some extra help. This extra help doesn't make the pupil "weird," nor does it mean that he or she is a "loser," any more than deaf or blind pupils should be considered weird or losers if they receive extra help in school. These adjustments should be looked at as part of the pupil's normal, regular school experience.

This chapter will try to help you understand which changes will often be made in the education of dyslexic pupils, and why these changes are logical and necessary.

TAKING TESTS

Everyone in school takes tests. Every week you take tests to see if you learned your spelling words, to see if you understood long division or fractions, or to see if you studied your science or social studies assignment. And once a year, you take a week of big standardized tests. On these tests, you mark the right meaning of words, you tell where commas and capital letters are missing from sentences, you pick out words that are spelled incorrectly, and you answer questions like "What's the best title for this story?"

Pupils with learning disabilities usually find these tests very hard. They have trouble reading the words on the test, so they're not sure which words to mark. They read slowly, so they don't have enough time to finish the test. They know they'll probably get a low score, so they come to fear and hate tests more than the rest of us do.

Because of their learning problems, dyslexic pupils take other special tests as well. When something goes wrong with your car, you take it to a mechanic to have it tested by an expert. When you have a pain in your leg, you go to the doctor to see what's wrong. When things don't go well in school, dyslexic pupils have to take special tests to find out what's wrong. Pupils with learning disabilities have to take more than their share of tests.

Diagnostic Tests

The special tests that are used with dyslexic pupils are not the type that you pass or fail or get a grade on. Most of these tests are called *diagnostic* tests. Diagnosis is finding out more about a problem. If you have a cough, the doctor diagnoses that cough to see what's causing it and what to do about it. If a teacher suspects a pupil has dyslexia, then a specialist is called in to diagnose that problem, too.

What are the special tests that dyslexic pupils have to take? These tests usually include:

- a physical examination, to make sure that the pupil's learning problems are not due to poor eyesight, bad hearing, or poor health
- intelligence tests, which try to measure the pupil's mental ability
- perception tests, to see whether problems may be happening as information is flashed back and forth between the ears, eyes, hands, and brain
- language tests, to measure the pupil's ability to understand and to use language
- reading tests, to find out where special problems in reading occur

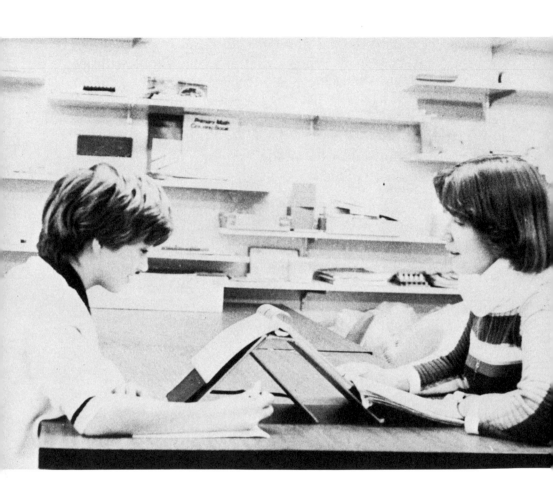

A child with dyslexia often has to take special tests. These tests help teachers find out exactly what's wrong with a pupil's reading and writing.

Samples of items from some of these tests are in the boxes on pages 62-3.

This may seem like a lot of testing, and indeed it is. But all of these tests are given for one reason: to get information that will be useful in helping the dyslexic pupil learn to read better.

Often, a whole team of experts gives these tests: teachers, specialists, doctors and nurses, psychologists, and others. The team usually has a captain who says which tests should be used and who explains the results afterward. Some of the tests may require special equipment, so they may be given in a hospital or a clinic. The tests are always given to pupils one at a time, not in a group.

Most dyslexic pupils don't like taking these tests. They feel fearful and nervous. Because the test is given to them individually, they can't guess or fake an answer. The tester keeps probing their weak spots, asking them to do what they have trouble doing. Taking the tests turns into a nightmare.

Often, these special tests that dyslexic pupils take confirm for the first time that the pupil has a learning disability. When they find out about the nature of their learning problem, different pupils react differently. The first reaction of some pupils is shock. They become extremely worried about the learning problem that the tests reveal.

Other pupils react differently. They are relieved to find out that they have dyslexia. These pupils know that they are intelligent, but that they still have problems learning to read and write. The tests help them understand a little more about the nature and cause of their problem. With this understanding, they are able to deal with the problem a little better than before.

For older dyslexic pupils and adults, special adjustments are often made in taking tests. Very often it is necessary to take a test to get into college, to get a job, or to get a

SOME TYPICAL ITEMS FROM
DIAGNOSTIC LEARNING TESTS

Here are examples of test questions or items that are used to measure a person's perception or learning skills:

Question or Item	Purpose
"I am going to say two words at a time. You tell me if the words I say are the same or different:	To find out if you can tell differences between sounds in words
cab cap *stone store*"	
"I am going to say three numbers in a row. Can you repeat the three numbers when I am finished? *6 . . . 2 . . . 3*"	To find out how well you can remember information that you hear
"When I say a word, you say a word with the opposite meaning: *dry*"	To find out if you know the meaning of words
"I'm going to show you three shapes. Then I'm going to take them away."	To find out if you can remember what you see

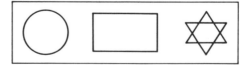

Question or Item   **Purpose**

"Show me the cat. Point to   To find out if you know the
the picture of something you   names and uses of objects
would sit on."

"Draw a line between these
two dots."

"Copy this shape."

     To find out if information is
                        going properly from your eye
                        to your brain to your hand

"See if you can draw this figure from memory."

"Find the part missing from   To find out if you can see rela-
this figure."   tionships between objects

Many, many other different types of items are also used.

These test questions may seem very easy to you. That's because
only very simple examples were used here. On real tests, the
questions and items are a lot harder. They can be especially hard for a
child with a perceptual problem or with a learning disability.

promotion in your job. These tests are usually written, and they have to be finished in a short time. Because of reading and other learning problems, dyslexic people often don't do well on these tests. These people are often intelligent and know the answers. But they can't read the material, organize the information, or answer the questions quickly enough.

Gradually, adjustments are being made for learning-disabled people in taking tests like this. Dyslexic people are being allowed more time than the average person to take the test. With more time, their scores generally get better. This is allowing more dyslexic students to get into college, where they often do very well.

Some people say that giving dyslexic students more time to finish a test is not fair. But these people would not expect a student with no hands to write a test. The dyslexic's problem with reading is no less real than the handicap of the person with no hands.

Not long ago, a policeman who has dyslexia took a written exam for a promotion. Because of his reading and writing problems, he failed the test by a few points even though he knew most of the material on the test. Then he won the right to take the test orally. He not only passed the test; he got the highest score in the group. Thus he was not denied the promotion because of his reading and writing problems. He earned the promotion because of his knowledge and skills.

Adjustments in these tests are being made to allow dyslexic people to use the talents they have to the best of their abilities, in spite of their problems with reading and writing.

LEARNING HOW TO READ

People learn to read in many different ways. You may have learned to read the stories in your first grade book by looking at the words and saying them over and over again. The teacher probably taught you to sound out some of these words, too. Or you may have told stories to the teacher, who wrote these stories down for you to read. You may have used tapes, games, computers, or other devices in learning how to read. There are over 150 different reading programs being used in schools today. And with all of them, dyslexic pupils have trouble learning how to read.

Reading is a difficult job for a dyslexic child. Remember, in Chapter 2, dyslexia was sometimes defined as a reading problem. Printed language gives the dyslexic child a lot of trouble. Often, dyslexic children can recognize the popular symbols they see around them. They recognize the golden arches that they see at McDonald's, traffic signals like stop signs, or the special lettering on cereal boxes. They have a lot more trouble, however, learning to recognize the symbols that make up their written language.

The first step in learning to read is learning the letters of the alphabet. For the dyslexic child, this can be difficult because a letter like *b* can look like *d* or *p*. They quickly get confused. The pupil can see the letters all right, but the look of the letter doesn't register correctly in the pupil's brain. So the teacher may use letters made from sandpaper or from Play Dough so that the pupil can feel as well as see the shape of the letters. By touching these rough letters, the pupil uses another path to get the information into his or her brain.

Problems with Reading

The dyslexic child usually begins reading in a group like everyone else in first grade. At first, when there are only a few words to remember, dyslexic pupils usually do as well as everyone else in the group. But as the stories get longer and there are more and more words to remember, reading becomes more and more difficult. There seems to be an invisible barrier inside the child's head blocking the words from getting in there. Pupils try hard, but they just can't remember what the words on the page say and mean. So they fall further and further behind in their reading group.

Failure in reading very often puzzles the dyslexic child. He or she has probably never had as much trouble learning anything before. These pupils come to school ready to succeed. As they encounter problems learning to read, they begin to doubt themselves and think that they might be "stupid." They may have enjoyed stories as little children, but now they hate to read.

That's when the teacher may give the dyslexic pupil another reading book, one that will work better and help the pupil learn. The sentences in the new reading book may be shorter and the words easier to sound out. The book itself may not be any easier to read, but it meets the needs of the dyslexic pupil.

A Special Approach

Sometimes, special reading programs are used with dyslexic pupils. The best known of these special programs is the Orton-Gillingham method. Dr. Samuel Orton spent a lifetime studying and treating children with specific language disabilities. Ms. Anne Gillingham was a teacher who developed special techniques based on Dr. Orton's theories. Their special method of teaching reading was invented especially for dyslexic pupils.

How is the Orton-Gillingham method different from other ways of teaching reading? First, it uses a multisensory approach. Because dyslexic pupils often have trouble with visual or auditory learning, touch and movement are also used. The method is sometimes called the VAKT technique. Words are taught through Visual (sight), Auditory (hearing), Kinesthetic (movement), and Tactual (touching or feeling) experience. Thus, the method tries to take advantage of all the strengths that the pupil has. It teaches letters and words by using as many pathways as possible to the pupil's brain. For any pupil, this multisensory approach can be useful. For learning-disabled pupils, it is often essential.

Learning to read with the Orton-Gillingham method is usually a slow, step-by-step process. The pupil learns letters and sounds by seeing and saying and tracing and copying and writing letters. When the letters and sounds are learned, the pupil learns to blend these into words. For example, the teacher shows the pupil three letter cards with one letter on each card: p i g, and the pupil has to put all the sounds together into the word *pig*. There's a lot of spelling and writing words as well.

The Orton-Gillingham program is not the only way that learning-disabled pupils learn how to read. There are other reading programs that have been used successfully as well. But the Orton-Gillingham method has worked with many dyslexic readers, and it is the one most widely known.

The Importance of Reading

For the dyslexic pupil not being able to read well is a serious handicap. Most of the time in the first three grades is spent learning to read and write. Thus, the pupil faces a major problem every school day. Reading becomes more important in the later grades. Pupils have to read their science and social studies books. They have to write reports and answer questions on exams. Because of their reading disability, their grades suffer in all subjects.

Reading problems also cause embarrassment in school. We all get embarrassed when we have to do what we're not good at doing. We get doubly embarrassed when somebody else is watching us. The dyslexic pupil is always called upon to do what he or she is not good at doing. The problems and weaknesses are always pointed out. School becomes an unhappy place.

Children's problems are made worse when classmates laugh at or make fun of them because of their learning problems. Many dyslexic pupils say that the teasing is what they hate most about school. They are intelligent and normal in all other ways, and so they are frustrated and baffled at their troubles in learning to read and write. The teasing or ridicule of classmates makes the hurt even worse.

If reading is so important, how do dyslexic people get along without it? Because they are intelligent, most dyslexic pupils and adults try to hide their reading problems. They go to the library and take out books, even though they can't read these books. They get a brother, a sister, or a friend they can trust to help them with work that requires reading and writing. They watch the news on TV so that they will be able to talk about what's going on in the world. They make excuses when reading assignments are not done. They listen carefully as friends discuss books that these friends have read. Then they are able to talk about the books and sound as if they've read them, too. They remember other symbols or signs instead of reading words in places like movie theaters and supermarkets. They let someone else order their food in restaurants because they may not be able to read the menu.

In many cases, dyslexic people use every means that they can to avoid reading. Some dyslexics seek help for their problems. Others go through life hiding the fact that they cannot read and hoping no one else will discover that fact.

Extra Help

Besides sometimes using a different type of reading program, other changes may have to be made in the classroom routine to help the dyslexic pupil. Once again, it's important to remember that these changes are necessary because of the dyslexic pupil's disability. A deaf pupil in the classroom will need someone to communicate in sign language. A dyslexic pupil in the classroom may need some adjustments as well.

Dyslexic pupils often need a "buddy" to help with spoken or written directions. One of the problems that can be part of dyslexia is trouble understanding, organizing, and remembering directions. So when the teacher says, "Take out your blue workbooks, go to the table in the corner, open your books to page sixty-three, and do all the odd numbers," these directions can "short-circuit" the pupil's whole listening system. The buddy is someone who helps the pupil when he or she doesn't understand directions or doesn't understand what he or she is supposed to do.

Reading and writing assignments may sometimes have to be changed. Dyslexic pupils cannot read as well, as fast, or as much as their classmates. So they need to use other ways of getting information. For example, the class is studying elections. The teacher gives groups an assignment to prepare reports. Most of the pupils use newspapers, magazines, encyclopedias, and other reference books to get information for their reports.

Because of their reading disabilities, the teacher lets the dyslexic pupils gather information in another way. These pupils talk to their parents and neighbors about elections. They conduct their own polls. They gather advertisements that the candidates put out. They even interview some of the candidates and their managers. Although they don't use printed materials, they get a lot of information about elections. They learn a lot. They share this information in discussions and in oral reports with the rest of the class. They do not pay a penalty because of their problems with print.

Pretend you fall down and break your arm. Your hand, the one you use to write, is in a cast. You can't hold a pencil or a pen. There's a big exam the next day. You know all the answers, but you can't write. Do you think it would be fair for the teacher to make you take the test by writing the answers?

That's the same kind of problem dyslexics often face in the classroom. They often know all the information on a test or a quiz. But because of their learning disability, they have trouble writing down the information that is in their head. That's why the dyslexic pupils in the classroom are often allowed to dictate or say their test answers rather than write them.

The same is true for stories, reports, and other writing assignments. Dyslexic pupils can sometimes use a tape recorder, a typewriter, or a word processor to help them get their ideas out. This is the same kind of adjustment that would be right for other handicapped pupils. It's the type of adjustment that should often be made for the pupil with learning disabilities.

Some experts argue against letting dyslexic pupils use speech rather than print all the time on assignments and exams. These authorities claim that avoiding reading and writing is not a fair way of helping learning-disabled pupils deal with their problems. In high school, pupils have to read and write much more. And after high school, they enter a world filled with print.

Few teachers, however, suggest that dyslexic pupils never be exposed to print in school. These teachers let the pupils use speech instead of reading and writing while they are

Computers can help dyslexic learners with schoolwork. But sometimes there are problems—finding the right keys, remembering what to do, and reading the print on the screen.

building the basics that they need. Dyslexic pupils often need this break while they are building skill, confidence, and other areas of strength to go on to become successful students and adults. This extra help that dyslexic pupils receive doesn't make them "stupid" or "weird." It just gives them an equal chance to succeed.

Resource Rooms

In regular classrooms, even the very best teachers often do not have the time to give learning-disabled pupils the extra help and individual attention they need. So most schools have resource rooms where dyslexic pupils can go for special help. In these resource rooms, teachers who understand the learning problems of dyslexic pupils work with these pupils to help them deal with difficulties they meet in school.

What goes on in a resource room? Nothing magical or secret happens there. Pupils work at their own level. For example, a fourth grade pupil may be reading at a first grade level. In a resource room, the pupil gets books that he or she can read and understand. There's usually a heavy emphasis on reading and spelling. Sometimes this is where pupils learn the Orton-Gillingham method of reading. There may also be help in other school subjects. For example, the resource room teacher may help the pupil do an outline or take notes for a report in science.

Because dyslexia is a perceptual problem, resource room teachers also work on perceptual skills. Pupils do exercises and play games to help them perceive sounds and symbols better. All of these activities are indirectly related to reading and writing.

Within a resource room, groups are usually small. Teachers are specially trained to understand and to deal with pupils' problems. Teaching is tailor-made. Special equipment is

In resource rooms pupils work with blocks and other objects. Working with shapes and colors helps pupils remember what different forms look like, improving their perceptual skills.

often available. Special projects are done to try to make learning fun. The dyslexic pupil has a better chance to succeed.

In spite of all these advantages, however, most pupils do not like going to a resource room. They don't want to be different. They would rather be in the classroom with their friends. They don't like the stigma or image because they have to go to a special room. They don't like missing out on the activities in the classroom. They don't like the extra work they have to do. But most of all, learning-disabled pupils don't like to be teased about having to go for extra help. Other children call them names. Classmates make fun of them because of a problem that they can't help. Dyslexic pupils usually don't mind the resource room as much as they mind the reactions of others when they go there.

Often when dyslexic pupils go on to high school, they need to use resource rooms as well. In high school, pupils have a lot more reading and writing to do. Learning-disabled pupils have an uphill battle. Resource room teachers help them with their reading and writing assignments. Resource room teachers try to help other teachers understand pupils' learning problems.

FURTHER EDUCATION

High school can be the turning point of the dyslexic pupil's life. It is here that the students learn to cope with the demands of school in spite of their learning problems. Here the students learn to use strengths to overcome weaknesses. Here they learn to succeed. With success in high school, it is likely that the students will go on to success in college.

Sometimes dyslexic pupils go to special schools. These

schools have different programs especially for learning-disabled students. Classes are usually small and all the students understand one another's problems. No one is different because he or she needs extra help or tutoring. These schools are set up to meet the unique needs of the dyslexic pupil. They try to provide special programs to prepare the student for college.

Many dyslexic learners go to college. In college they still need extra help in their work. Special learning centers are available to help them with reading and writing. Special counselors advise them about which courses to take. Often, tutors work with them. College friends help out a lot, too. College can sometimes be difficult for the dyslexic student, but it can also be fun. Most dyslexic students who go to college graduate and go on to successful lives.

WHAT ABOUT DRUGS?

This chapter has dealt with teaching and other educational treatments for dyslexia and learning problems. That is, the problem is treated by teaching reading and writing in a special way and by making adjustments in the pupil's school program. But we often hear about the use of drugs and medicines to solve a child's learning problems. What about drugs as a cure for dyslexia?

Dyslexia, remember, is not a disease. It's not a condition that can be cured by drugs. When doctors prescribe drugs to children with learning difficulties, the drugs are often used to remedy the conditions attached to a learning problem. The drugs are not, however, designed to cure the learning problem itself. For example, if a child is constantly moving and has a lot of trouble paying attention, drugs may be prescribed to help the child settle down. Being more quiet, the pupil will be able to pay attention better and to learn more. The medicine itself is not, however, what makes the child learn more. Drugs may indirectly influence learning, but they do not directly cause learning to happen.

There was a time when more people believed in giving drugs to dyslexic learners. Some still believe in the use of drugs. But because of side effects, most experts are becoming more cautious. They have come to realize that drugs can't help a child learn to read and write.

Perhaps in the future, when we learn more about dyslexia and its causes, a drug may be invented that will help the dyslexic person learn more easily. But for now, the best treatment seems to be a good school program.

Chapter **5**

The Dyslexia "Problem"

There is a famous old folk tale from India about six blind men and an elephant. The story is that the six men wanted to find out what an elephant looked like. Being blind, they had to find out by touching the animal.

One man felt the elephant's side and said, "The elephant is big like a wall." A second man felt the smooth, sharp tusk and declared, "The elephant is shaped like a spear." A third, who felt the leg, said, "No, the elephant is more like a tree." A fourth felt the elephant's ear and said that the elephant was like a soft, leafy fan. A fifth man felt the tail and said the elephant felt like a rope. The sixth blind man felt the elephant's trunk and said, "The elephant is shaped like a snake."

In one way, each man was correct. Yet all together, they were wrong.

What does this old Indian folk tale have to do with dyslexia? People, when they talk about dyslexia, are like the six blind men trying to describe the elephant. They describe part of the problem, mostly the part with which they are most directly concerned.

Some experts talk about dyslexia as a medical problem. They believe that the source of the problem is the composition of the brain or a fault somewhere in the central nervous system. These experts provide treatment to improve perceptual skills.

Other experts see dyslexia as an educational problem. Dyslexia is a problem that directly involves reading and writing, so these people provide different types of instruction to help improve these basic educational skills.

Another group is more concerned with the psychological aspects of dyslexia, the psychological and emotional distress that results from failure and frustration. These people deal with the psychological effects that the learning problem produces.

Many ordinary people look at the social impact of dyslexia. They point to the thousands and thousands of students who graduate from high school every year barely able to read and write. They point to the millions of people in society who are functionally illiterate; that is, people who cannot read well enough to meet basic needs like applying for a job or reading a newspaper. Society places demands on its citizens to read and write. If there were no written language, dyslexia would not be a problem. The American Indian of the distant past who could shoot a straight arrow and quickly skin a buffalo didn't have to suffer because of dyslexia. But as society becomes more technologically advanced, the need to deal with print becomes more important.

Lots of people look at the financial problems of dyslexia. The U.S. government spends millions of dollars a year on special education. So do state governments. School systems spend more millions of dollars on people and programs for disabled learners in school. Parents who send their dyslexic children to private schools spend more money as well. The financial impact is even greater when one considers the lost wages that dyslexic adults suffer because they can't get a job or can't get promoted in their jobs because they can't write well enough. Dyslexia costs the American public millions of dollars a year.

Like the six blind men, looking at different aspects of dyslexia does not give an idea of the whole problem. The medical, educational, psychological, social, and financial aspects of the problem don't tell the whole story. Dyslexia is, most important of all, a *human* problem.

Dyslexia is the problem of people who are talented but whose problems with reading and writing keep these talents from showing. It's the problem of people who often get telephone numbers all mixed up in their heads. It's the problem of people who are afraid to leave their hotel rooms in a strange town because they are afraid they will get lost trying to figure out the way back to the hotel. It's the problem of people who go through school thinking that they are really stupid when the real problem has not been recognized. Figures and statistics don't tell the story of dyslexia. People do.

A Final Note from the Author

In gathering information for this book, I talked to many people. Some of the people I interviewed had dyslexia themselves. Others were teachers or parents of dyslexic students.

At each interview, I asked people this question: "If you could give the world one important message about dyslexia, what would the message be?" Each person had a different answer, but all the answers were amazingly similar. They all had one theme: *People with dyslexia can succeed.*

The specific messages can be summarized like this: Dyslexics can learn to read and write. It takes time. It takes work. But they can succeed. In fact, they can *exceed.* And when they do become successful, their experiences will make them better, more understanding people.

Dyslexia is a real problem that people have. But it is not a reason not to be successful. Dyslexics may have to work harder than other people, but they can use their strengths and talents to become a success.

These are messages from people who deal with dyslexia every day!

Appendixes

Appendix A

Public Law 94-142: It's the Law!

For many years, schools have had special education for pupils with special needs. These special services have usually included separate classes for children with serious handicaps, remedial teachers or tutors for children with less serious learning difficulties, and other programs for children who had other school problems.

In some schools, however, no special programs were available. And even where some of these services were provided, lots of parents felt that not enough help was given. Many other parents felt that the right kind of services were not available, especially for children with dyslexia and other learning disabilities. And in most states, there was no law that demanded or required that these services be provided at all.

In 1975, the Congress of the United States changed all that. Congress passed a law about the education of handicapped children, including children with dyslexia. The law is called Public Law 94-142. It is meant to make sure that all children receive an education that is planned according to their own special needs.

Public Law 94-142 says:

> Children with learning problems—including dyslexia—have
> the right to a free public education and that this education

must meet their special learning needs. This right is for all people from the age of three until the age of twenty-two.

- Their education has to be based on a full assessment and evaluation of their special needs. Children must be fully tested to find out as much as possible about their learning problems before a program is planned.

- Every child who receives special services in schools must have a plan or program that is especially designed for him or her. This plan is called an Individualized Educational Program, or IEP for short. The IEP must say what special services the child will receive as part of his or her education.

- The child's parents have the right to know all about the program and to approve the evaluation and the education of their child. Every parent has the right to take part in every major decision that influences the education of his or her child.

- Handicapped children have to be educated as much as possible with non-handicapped children. Whenever possible, special-needs children, no matter how serious their problems may be, must be brought into the "mainstream" of school life with other children.

If parents think that the school is not giving their children the right kind of education, Public Law 94-142 gives the parents the right to appeal. First, parents can discuss their concerns with their child's teacher and others who work with their child. Then they can have a meeting with the school administrators. Finally, if they are still not satisfied, they can go to court if necessary.

Before 1975, some states already had laws about how special-needs children should be educated. For example, Massachusetts had a law called Chapter 766, which was about the education of children with dyslexia and other learning problems. But Public Law 94-142 was the first *federal* law passed to give children these educational rights. Now the law applies to children in all fifty states. All have the right to an education especially designed to meet their learning needs.

Appendix B

Organizations Concerned with Dyslexia

A number of societies and organizations are concerned with helping dyslexic people. These groups provide information and other materials to teachers, to parents of children with learning disabilities, and to dyslexics themselves. Some of these organizations are:

Orton Dyslexia Society. The organization most directly concerned with the education of dyslexic students is the Orton Dyslexia Society. Founded in 1949, the society is named after Dr. Samuel Orton, who made the study of dyslexia his life's work.

The Orton Dyslexia Society is dedicated to "the study and treatment of the specific language disability known as dyslexia." It tries to help people understand dyslexia and to encourage the right type of education for dyslexic pupils in school.

People can get more information about the Orton Dyslexia Society by writing to the organization at 724 York Road, Baltimore, MD 21204.

Foundation for Children with Learning Disabilities (FCLD). Established in 1977, this foundation has two major purposes: (1) to raise public awareness about dyslexia and related learning disabilities, and (2) to provide funds for projects and programs that serve children with learning disabilities.

FCLD's main job is to make people more aware about the problems that people with learning disabilities face every day. The organization does this by publishing a magazine and other excellent materials. These materials contain information on programs and services for dyslexic people, as well as information to make people more aware of the whole area of learning disabilities.

The address of the Foundation for Children with Learning Disabilities is 99 Park Avenue, New York, NY 10016.

Association for Children and Adults with Learning Disabilities (ACLD). This association was founded in 1964 by a group of parents of learning-disabled children. Members now include parents, teachers, learning-disabled adults, and others. ACLD is devoted to defining and finding solutions for the broad field of learning problems. The group provides information, plans programs, runs conferences, and sponsors laws about children with learning disabilities.

ACLD's headquarters are at 4156 Library Road, Pittsburgh, PA 15234.

Council for Exceptional Children (CEC). The Council for Exceptional Children is a professional organization. While its members are mostly teachers, CEC also has parents and other school workers who are concerned with improving the life of all exceptional learners, including dyslexic children. The organization works to protect the rights of people with special needs in school, in jobs, and in life.

The offices of the Council for Exceptional Children are located at 1920 Association Drive, Reston, VA 22091.

Index

ABOUT THE AUTHOR

John F. Savage has been a teacher for over twenty-five years. He has taught in the United States, in Canada, and in Europe. He graduated from Iona College and received a doctorate from Boston University. He is now a professor at Boston College in Chestnut Hill, Massachusetts.

Dr. Savage has written four books for teachers, eight programs for classrooms, and many articles for magazines and newspapers.